2021 Copyright © Bahá'í International Community
(www.bahai.org)

Designed and Published by Simon Creedy
(simon@creedy.com.au)

WORDS OF GOD

PRAYERS AND
HOLY WRITINGS
FROM

Bahá'u'lláh
The Báb
AND
'Abdu'l-Bahá

BAHÁ'U'LLÁH (1817-1892)
THE DIVINE EDUCATOR

In the middle of the 19th century, God summoned Bahá'u'lláh– meaning the "Glory of God"–to deliver a new Revelation to humanity. For four decades thousands of verses, letters and books flowed from His pen. In His Writings, He outlined a framework for the development of a global civilization which takes into account both the spiritual and material dimensions of human life.

I have never aspired after worldly leadership. My sole purpose hath been to hand down unto men that which I was bidden to deliver by God...

– Bahá'u'lláh

Bahá'u'lláh suffered 40 years of imprisonment, torture and exile for bringing God's latest message to humanity. Today, His life and mission are becoming increasingly well-known across the planet. Millions of people are learning to apply His teachings to their individual and collective lives for the betterment of the world.

The Shrine of Bahá'u'lláh, located in Bahjí near Akka, Israel, is the holiest place for Bahá'ís and represents their Qiblih, or direction of prayer. It contains the remains of Bahá'u'lláh and is near the spot where He died in the Mansion of Bahjí.

2021 Copyright © Bahá'í International Community (www.bahai.org)

THE BÁB (1819-1850)
HERALD OF THE BAHÁ'Í FAITH

In the middle of the 19th century–one of the most turbulent periods in the world's history–a young merchant announced that He was the bearer of a message destined to transform the life of humanity. At a time when His country, Iran, was undergoing widespread moral breakdown, His message aroused excitement and hope among all classes, rapidly attracting thousands of followers. He took the name "The Báb", meaning "the Gate" in Arabic.

With His call for spiritual and moral reformation, and His attention to improving the position of women and the lot of the poor, the Báb's prescription for spiritual renewal was revolutionary. At the same time, He founded a distinct, independent religion of His own, inspiring His followers to transform their lives and carry out great acts of heroism.

The Báb announced that humanity stood at the threshold of a new era. His mission, which was to last only six years, was to prepare the way for the coming of a Manifestation of God Who would usher in the age of peace and justice promised in all the world's religions: Bahá'u'lláh.

Shrine of The Báb, Mount Carmel, Haifa, Israel

2021 Copyright © Bahá'í International Community (www.bahai.org)

'ABDU'L-BAHÁ (1844-1921)
THE PERFECT EXEMPLAR

In the early years of the 20th century, 'Abdu'l-Bahá—the eldest Son of Bahá'u'lláh—was the Bahá'í Faith's leading exponent, renowned as a champion of social justice and an ambassador for international peace.

Upholding unity as the fundamental principle of His teachings, Bahá'u'lláh established the necessary safeguard to ensure that His religion would never suffer the same fate as others that split into sects after the deaths of their Founders. In His Writings, He instructed all to turn to His eldest Son, 'Abdu'l-Bahá, not only as the authorized interpreter of the Bahá'í Writings but also as the perfect exemplar of the Faith's spirit and teachings.

Following Bahá'u'lláh's passing, 'Abdu'l-Bahá's extraordinary qualities of character, His knowledge and His service to humanity offered a vivid demonstration of Bahá'u'lláh's teachings in action, and brought great prestige to the rapidly expanding community throughout the world.

'Abdu'l-Bahá devoted His ministry to furthering His Father's Faith and to promoting the ideals of peace and unity. He encouraged the establishment of local Bahá'í institutions, and guided nascent educational, social and economic initiatives. After His release from a lifetime of imprisonment, 'Abdu'l-Bahá set out on a series of journeys which took Him to Egypt, Europe and North America. Throughout His life, He presented with brilliant simplicity, to high and low alike, Bahá'u'lláh's prescription for the spiritual and social renewal of society.

Shrine of 'Abdu'l-Bahá close to the Ridván Garden in Akka, Israel

2021 Copyright © Bahá'í International Community (www.bahai.org)

Is there any Remover of difficulties save God? Say: Praised be God! He is God! All are His servants, and all abide by His bidding!

The Báb

O God, my God!

I yield Thee
thanks for having
guided me unto Thy straight Path
and enabled me to recognize
Thee and turn unto Thee, and for
having made known unto me the
oneness of Thine Essence and
the sanctity of Thy Being.
I implore Thee, by them Who
are the Daysprings of Thy Cause,
the Dawning-Places of Thy
grace, and the Repositories of
Thy knowledge and wisdom, to
bless the gift which Thou hast
bestowed upon me through
Thy bounty and favour.
Do Thou ordain for me and for
her mother, as well as for her, the
good of this world and of the next.
Thou art, verily, the Lord of all
being, Who hearest and
art ready to answer.

Bahá'u'lláh

Revealed for the recipient on the occasion of the birth of his daughter

Thy name is my healing, O my God, and remembrance of Thee is my remedy. Nearness to Thee is my hope, and love for Thee is my companion. Thy mercy to me is my healing and my succor in both this world and the world to come. Thou, verily, art the All-Bountiful, the All-Knowing, the All-Wise.

Bahá'u'lláh

Create in me a pure heart, O my God, and renew a tranquil conscience within me, O my Hope!

Through the spirit of power confirm Thou me in Thy Cause, O my Best-Beloved, and by the light of Thy glory reveal unto me Thy path, O Thou the Goal of my desire!

Through the power of Thy transcendent might lift me up unto the heaven of Thy holiness, O Source of my being, and by the breezes of Thine eternity gladden me, O Thou Who art my God! Let Thine everlasting melodies breathe tranquillity on me, O my Companion, and let the riches of Thine ancient countenance deliver me from all except Thee, O my Master, and let the tidings of the revelation of Thine incorruptible Essence bring me joy, O Thou Who art the most manifest of the manifest and the most hidden of the hidden!

Bahá'u'lláh

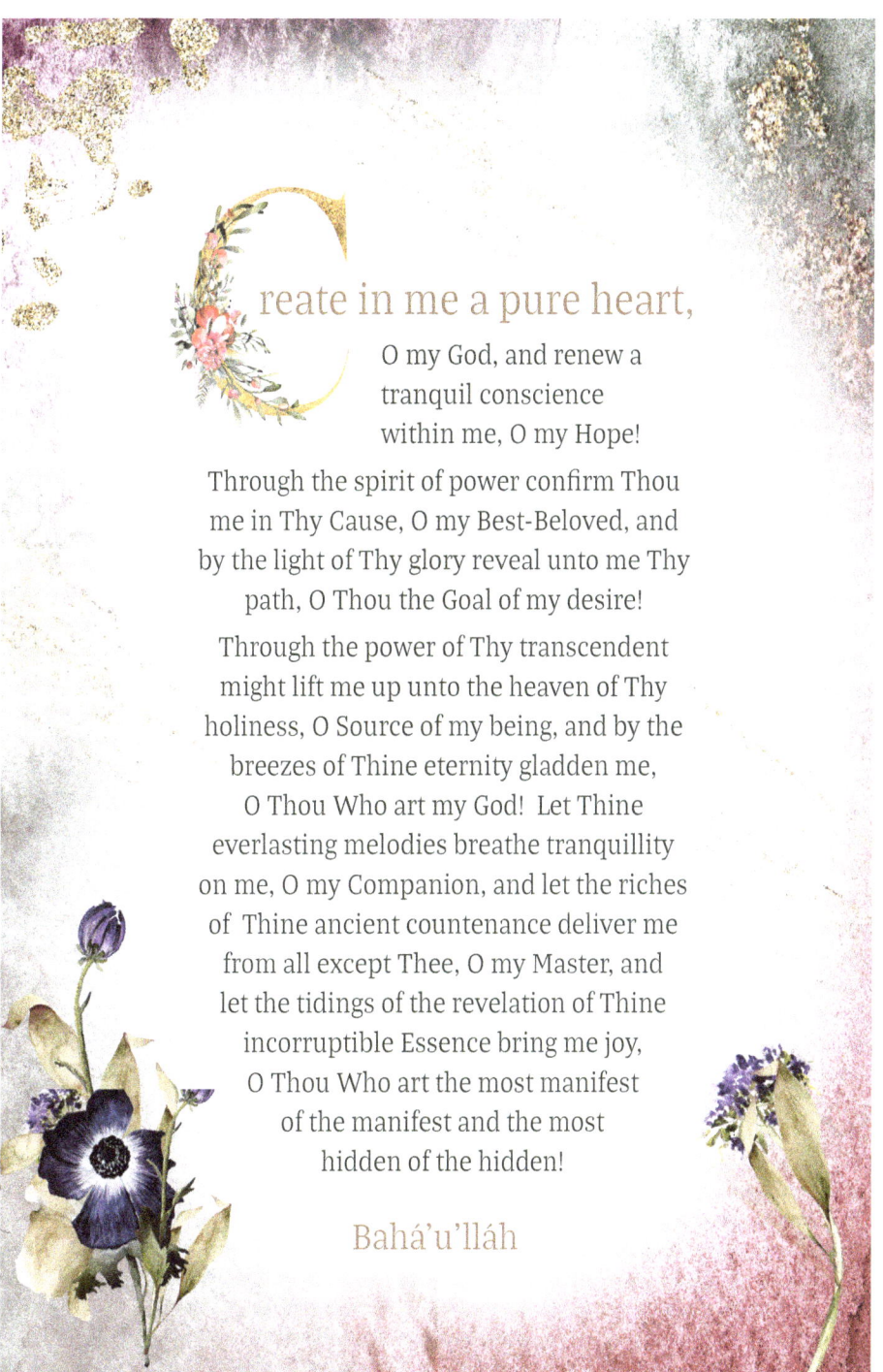

Blessed is the spot,
and the house,
and the place,
and the city,
and the heart,
and the mountain,
and the refuge,
and the cave,
and the valley,
and the land,
and the sea,
and the island,
and the meadow
where mention of God
hath been made,
and His praise
glorified.

Bahá'u'lláh

God,
guide me,
protect me,
make of me
a shining lamp
and a
brilliant star.
Thou art
the Mighty
and the
Powerful.

'Abdu'l-Bahá

My Lord! My Lord!

I praise Thee and thank Thee for the favour Thou hast bestowed upon this feeble handmaiden of Thine, Thy maidservant who is supplicating and praying fervently to Thee, inasmuch as Thou hast guided her unto Thy Straight Path, led her to Thy luminous Kingdom, inclined her ears to Thy most sublime Call in the midmost heart of the world, and unveiled to her eyes Thy signs which testify to the revelation of Thy supreme dominion over all things.

O my Lord! I dedicate that which is in my womb to Thee. Grant that this child may be praised in Thy Kingdom, may be blessed by Thy grace and bounty, and may grow and develop within the stronghold of Thine education. Verily, Thou art the Most Generous, the Lord of grace abounding.

'Abdu'l-Bahá

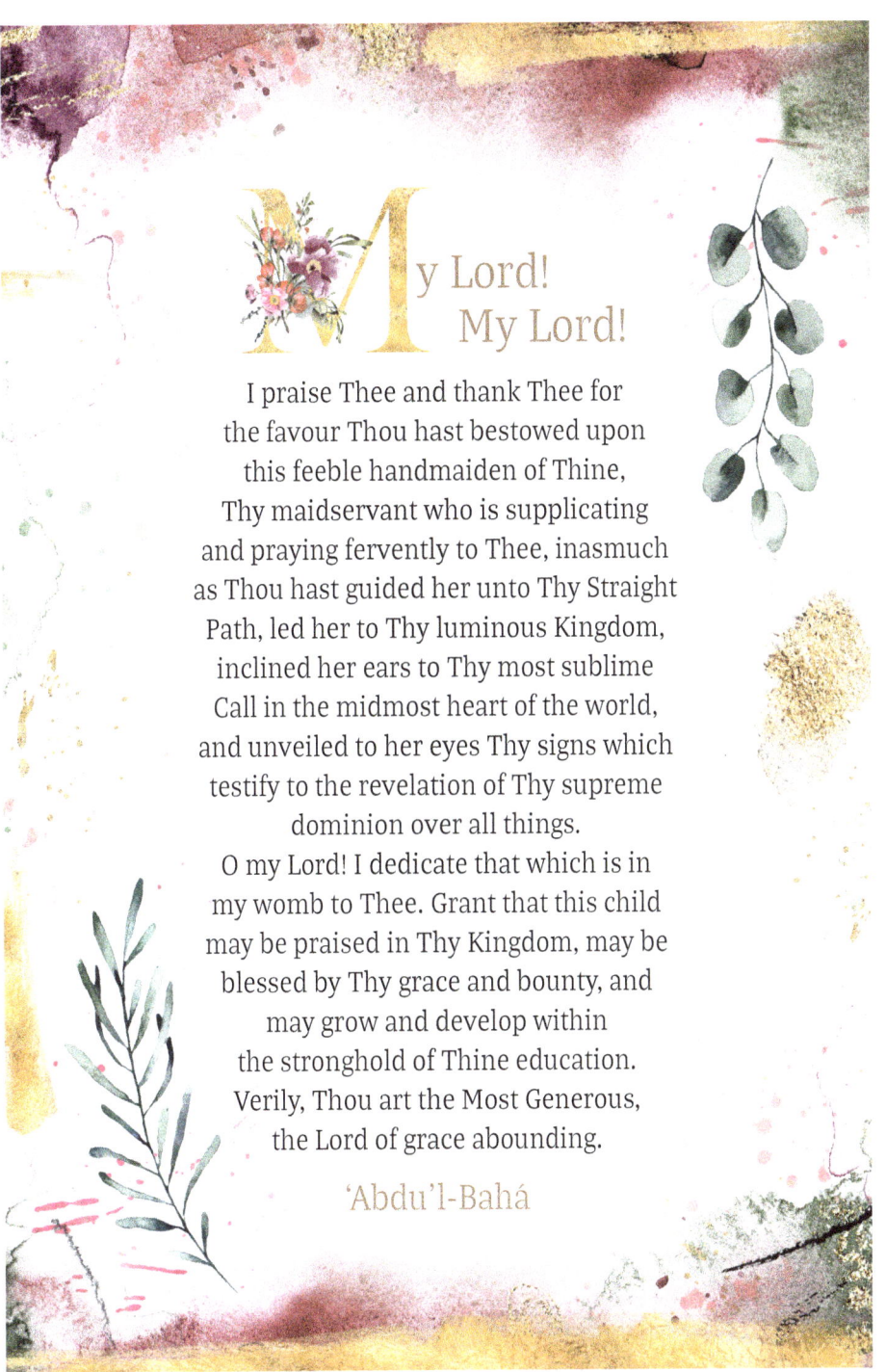

Make my prayer O my Lord, a fountain of living waters whereby I may live as long as Thy sovereignty endureth, and may make mention of Thee in every world of Thy worlds.

Bahá'u'lláh

Son of Being!

With the hands
of power
I made thee and
with the fingers
of strength
I created thee;
and within thee
have I placed
the essence of My light.
Be thou content with it
and seek naught else,
for My work is perfect
and My command
is binding.
Question it not,
nor have a
doubt thereof.

Bahá'u'lláh

Let us put aside all thoughts of self;
let us close our eyes
to all on earth,
let us neither
make known
our sufferings
nor complain of
our wrongs.
Rather let us
become oblivious
of our own selves,
and drinking down
the wine of
heavenly grace,
let us cry out our joy,
and lose ourselves
in the beauty
of the
All-Glorious.

'Abdu'l-Bahá

O Son of Spirit!

My first counsel is this: Possess a pure, kindly and radiant heart, that thine may be a sovereignty ancient, imperishable and everlasting.

Bahá'u'lláh

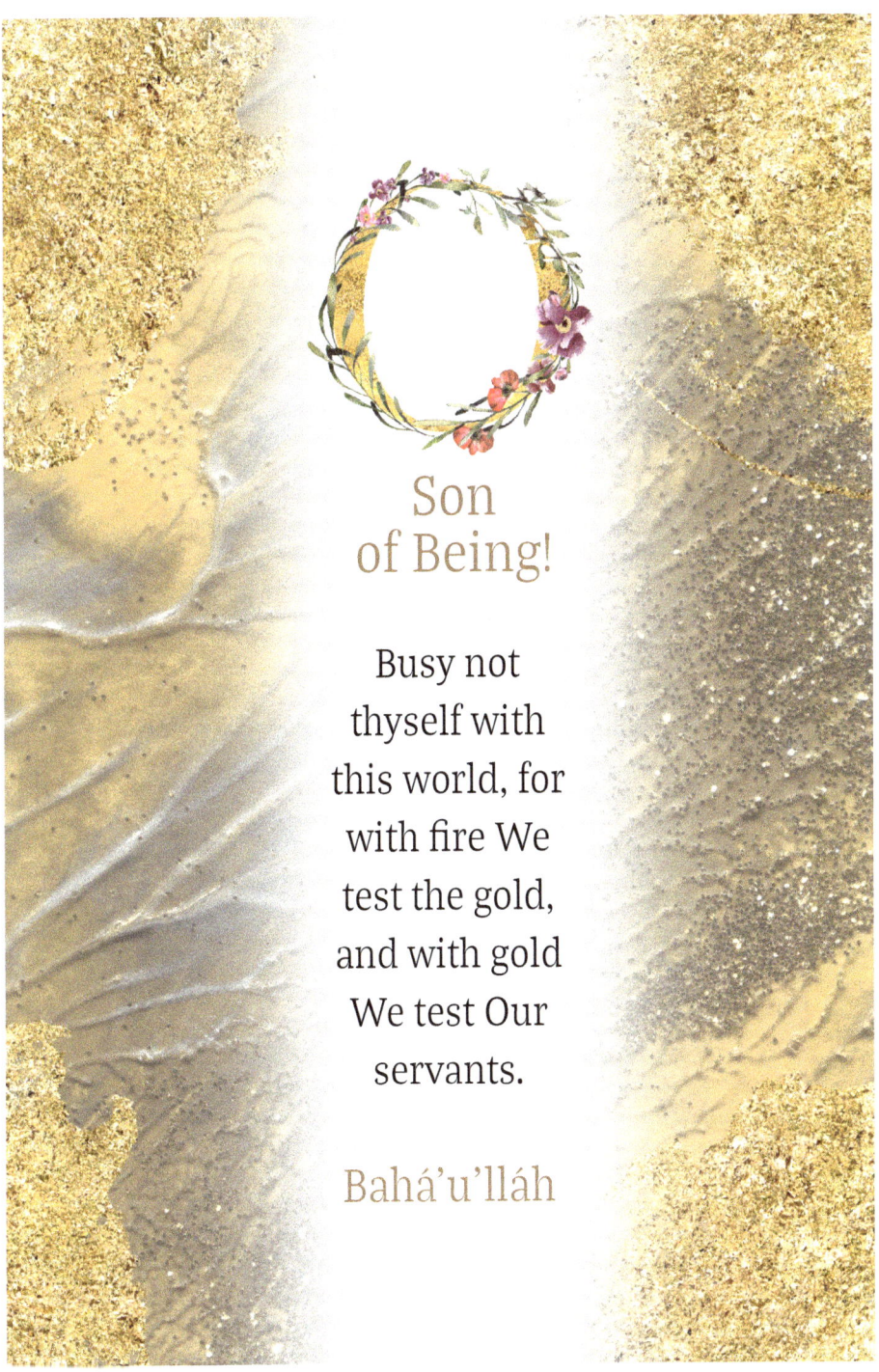

Son of Being!

Busy not thyself with this world, for with fire We test the gold, and with gold We test Our servants.

Bahá'u'lláh

O My Friend in Word!

Ponder awhile. Hast thou ever heard that friend and foe should abide in one heart? Cast out then the stranger, that the Friend may enter His home.

Bahá'u'lláh

Son of Being!

Love Me,
that I may
love thee.
If thou lovest
Me not,
My love can
in no wise
reach thee.
Know this,
O servant.

Bahá'u'lláh

Son of Man!

For everything there is a sign. The sign of love is fortitude under My decree and patience under My trials.

Bahá'u'lláh

O My Servant!

Free thyself from the fetters of this world, and loose thy soul from the prison of self. Seize thy chance, for it will come to thee no more.

Bahá'u'lláh

Man of Two Visions!

Close one eye
and open the other.
Close one to the world
and all that is therein,
and open the
other to the
hallowed beauty
of the Beloved.

Bahá'u'lláh

O Son of Justice!

Whither can a lover go but to the land of his beloved? and what seeker findeth rest away from his heart's desire? To the true lover reunion is life, and separation is death. His breast is void of patience and his heart hath no peace. A myriad lives he would forsake to hasten to the abode of his beloved.

Bahá'u'lláh

Son of Being!

Thou art My lamp and My light is in thee. Get thou from it thy radiance and seek none other than Me. For I have created thee rich and have bountifully shed My favour upon thee.

Bahá'u'lláh

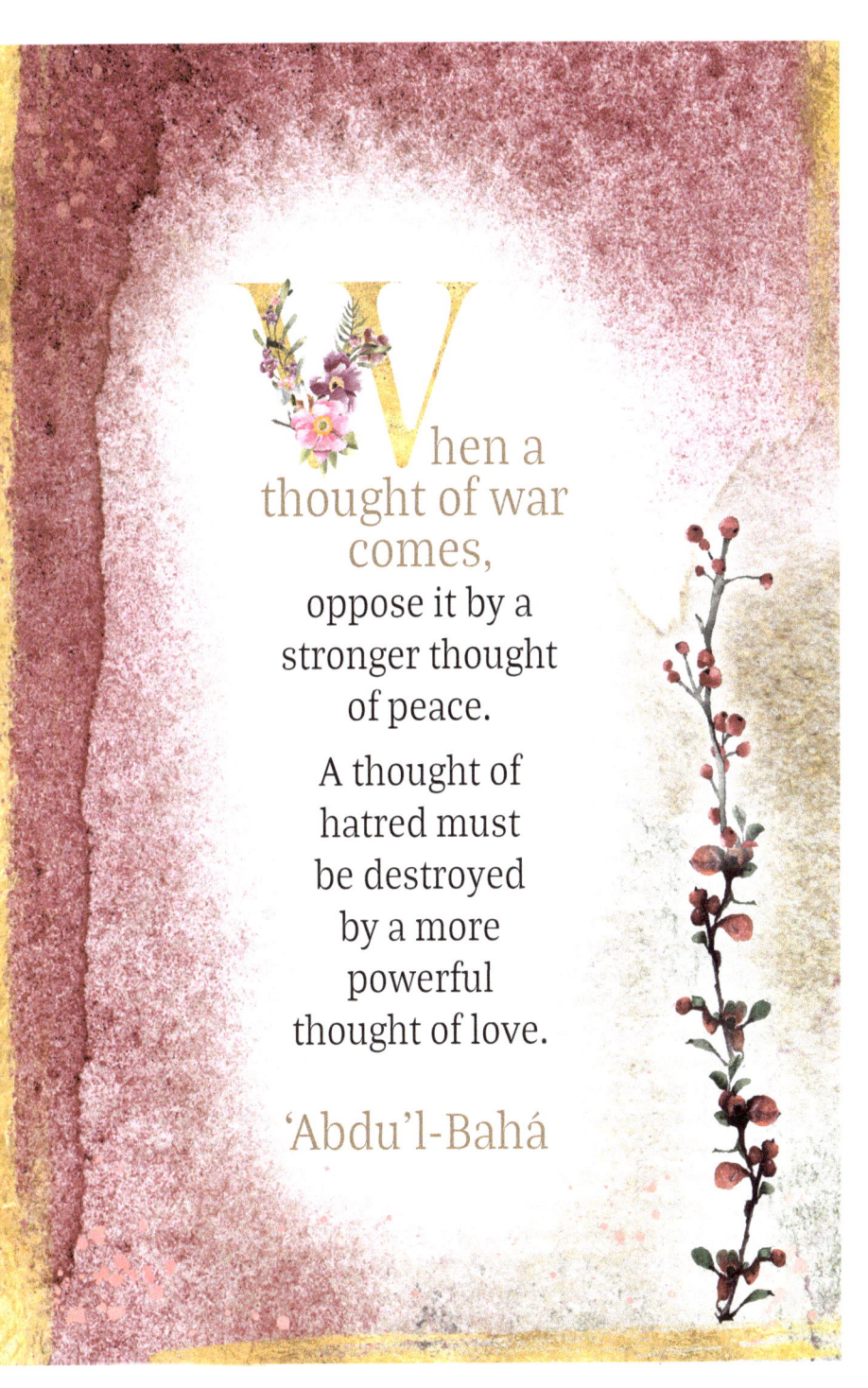

When a thought of war comes, oppose it by a stronger thought of peace.

A thought of hatred must be destroyed by a more powerful thought of love.

'Abdu'l-Bahá

Tablet of Visitation of 'Abdu'l-Bahá

Whoso reciteth this prayer with lowliness and fervor will bring gladness and joy to the heart of this Servant; it will be even as meeting Him face to face.

He is the All-Glorious!

O God, my God! Lowly and tearful, I raise my suppliant hands to Thee and cover my face in the dust of that Threshold of Thine, exalted above the knowledge of the learned, and the praise of all that glorify Thee. Graciously look upon Thy servant, humble and lowly at Thy door, with the glances of the eye of Thy mercy, and immerse him in the Ocean of Thine eternal grace. Lord! He is a poor and lowly servant of Thine, enthralled and imploring Thee, captive in Thy hand, praying fervently to Thee, trusting in Thee, in tears before Thy face, calling to Thee and beseeching Thee, saying: O Lord, my God! Give me Thy grace to serve Thy loved ones, strengthen me in my servitude to Thee, illumine my brow with the light of adoration in Thy court of holiness, and of prayer to Thy kingdom of grandeur. Help me to be selfless at the heavenly entrance of Thy gate, and aid me to be detached from all things within Thy holy precincts. Lord! Give me to drink from the chalice of selflessness; with its robe clothe me, and in its ocean immerse me. Make me as dust in the pathway of Thy loved ones, and grant that I may offer up my soul for the earth ennobled by the footsteps of Thy chosen ones in Thy path, O Lord of Glory in the Highest. With this prayer doth Thy servant call Thee, at dawntide and in the night-season. Fulfill his heart's desire, O Lord! Illumine his heart, gladden his bosom, kindle his light, that he may serve Thy Cause and Thy servants. Thou art the Bestower, the Pitiful, the Most Bountiful, the Gracious, the Merciful, the Compassionate.

'Abdu'l-Bahá

www.ingramcontent.com/pod-product-compliance
Lightning Source LLC
Chambersburg PA
CBHW040417100526
44588CB00022B/2861